Art & Helen
_____
To

Betty McNeil
_____
From

6 - 5 - 11
_____
Date

© 2010 by Barbour Publishing, Inc.

ISBN 978-1-61626-046-0

Cover and interior design: Kirk DouPonce, www.DogEaredDesign.com

Published by Barbour Publishing, Inc., P.O. Box 719, Uhrichsville, Ohio 44683, www.barbourbooks.com

Our mission is to publish and distribute inspirational products offering exceptional value and biblical encouragement to the masses.

 Member of the Evangelical Christian Publishers Association

Printed in Malaysia.

YOU ARE A

Blessing

BARBOUR
PUBLISHING

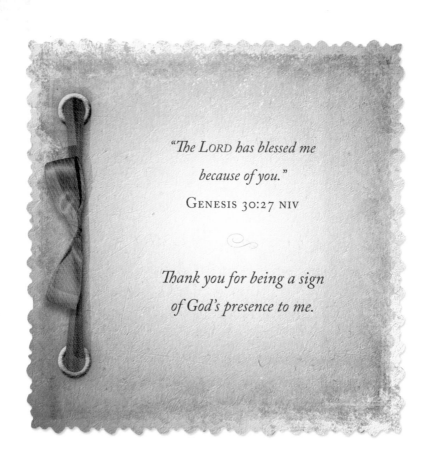

"The LORD has blessed me
because of you."

GENESIS 30:27 NIV

Thank you for being a sign
of God's presence to me.

Human beings ought to. . .
share all the gifts they have received from God.

MEISTER ECKHART

If you want your neighbor to see what God's spirit
will do for him, let him see what it has done for you.

HENRY WARD BEECHER

Thank you for sharing what God has given you!

Circle of Blessing

A circle has no beginning and no ending.
The circle of blessing can begin at any point
within it. The circle is made up of quiet actions,
love, simple gratitude, forgiveness, generous
gifts, trust, precious memories, a heart that
knows what to remember and what to forget.

ELLYN SANNA

Our duty is not to see through one another
but to see one another through.

LEONARD SWEET

❧

You should rely on love.

HADEWIJCH OF BRABANT

❧

Great opportunities to help others seldom come,
but small ones surround us daily.

SALLY KOCH

One day held the memory of you...

And sowed the sky with tiny clouds of love.

RUPERT BROOKE

I thank my God upon every remembrance of you.

PHILIPPIANS 1:3 KJV

I cannot but remember such things were,

That were most precious to me.

WILLIAM SHAKESPEARE

Love is a choice—
not simply or necessarily a rational choice,
but rather a willingness to be present to
others without pretense or guile.

CARTER HEYWARD

Keep love in your heart.
A life without it is like a sunless
garden when the flowers are dead.
The consciousness of loving and being
loved brings a warmth and richness
to life that nothing else can bring.

OSCAR WILDE

We do not make friends as we make houses,
but discover them as we do the arbutus, under the
leaves of our lives, concealed in our experience.

WILLIAM RADER

Every true friend is a glimpse of God.

LUCY LARCOM

One who knows how to show and to accept kindness
will be a friend better than any possession.

SOPHOCLES

It is only with the heart that one can see rightly;

what is essential is invisible to the eye.

ANTOINE DE SAINT-EXUPÉRY

For where your treasure is, there will your heart be also.

MATTHEW 6:21 KJV

The best and most beautiful things in the world cannot be seen or even touched. They must be felt with the heart.

HELEN KELLER

*Life is full of people who will make you laugh, cry,
smile until your face hurts, and so happy that you think
you'll burst. But the ones who leave their footprints on your
soul are the ones that keep your life going.*

NATALIE BERNOT

*When we honestly ask ourselves which person
in our lives means the most to us, we often
find that it is those who, instead of giving advice,
solutions, or cures, have chosen rather to share our pain
and touch our wounds with a warm and
tender hand. The friend who can be silent with us in a
moment of despair or confusion, who can stay with us
in an hour of grief and bereavement, who can tolerate
not knowing, not curing, not healing,
and face with us the reality of our powerlessness,
that is a friend who cares.*

HENRI NOUWEN

Friendship without self-interest is one of the rare and beautiful things in life.

JAMES FRANCIS BYRNES

There are two things one should know about the direction of his life. First is: Where am I going? Second is: Who will go with me?

ELIE WIESEL

God does notice us,

and He watches

over us. But it is usually

through another person

that He meets our needs.

SPENCER W. KIMBALL

The love we give away
is the only love we keep.

ELBERT HUBBARD

*It's sublime to feel and say of another...
I rely on him as on myself.*

RALPH WALDO EMERSON

He who sows courtesy reaps friendship,
and he who plants kindness gathers love.

SAINT BASIL

A heart in tune with God
is a heart that beats for others.

BONNIE JENSEN

So encourage each other and build each other up,

just as you are already doing.

1 THESSALONIANS 5:11 NLT

"Love thy neighbor" is a precept which could

transform the world if it were universally practiced.

MARY MCLEOD BETHUNE

We live by admiration, hope, and love.

WILLIAM WORDSWORTH

❧

Happiness is something to do,
something to love, something to hope for.

CHINESE PROVERB

❧

Joy is the net of love by which
you can catch souls.

MOTHER TERESA

Into all lives, in many simple, familiar, homely ways, God infuses this element of joy from the surprises of life, which unexpectedly brighten our days, and fill our eyes with light.

HENRY WADSWORTH LONGFELLOW

Every heart that has beat strong and cheerfully has left a hopeful impulse behind it in the world and bettered the tradition of mankind.

ROBERT LOUIS STEVENSON

*Blessed are those who give
without remembering
and receive without forgetting.*

BERNARD MELTZER

*Little deeds of kindness,
Little words of love,
Help to make earth happy,
Like the heaven above.*

J. FLETCHER CARNEY

*That action is best which procures the
greatest happiness for the greatest numbers.*

FRANCIS HUTCHESON

Friends are as companions on a journey
who ought to aid each other to persevere
in the road to a happier life.

PYTHAGORAS

If one falls down, his friend can help
him up. But pity the man who falls
and has no one to help him up!

ECCLESIASTES 4:10 NIV

The more we love, the better we are;
and the greater our friendships are,
the dearer we are to God.

JEREMY TAYLOR

Good company upon the road
is the shortest cut.

ANONYMOUS

A real friend helps us think our best thoughts,
do our noblest deeds, be our finest selves.

UNKNOWN

Friendship is unnecessary, like philosophy,
like art. . . . It has no survival value; rather it is one
of those things that gives value to survival.

C. S. LEWIS

*Those who bring sunshine to the lives
of others cannot keep it from themselves.*

JAMES M. BARRIE

*It is through kindness and compassion
that hearts connect. . . .*

BONNIE JENSEN

Familiar acts are beautiful through love.

PERCY BYSSHE SHELLEY

All God's angels
come to us disguised.

JAMES RUSSELL LOWELL

When you rise in the morning,
form a resolution to make the day
a happy one to a fellow friend.

SYDNEY SMITH

If instead of a gem,

or even a flower,

we should cast the gift

of a loving thought into

the heart of a friend,

that would be giving as

the angels give.

GEORGE MACDONALD

*As in filling a vessel drop by drop,
there is at last a drop which makes it run over,
so in a series of kindnesses there is,
at last, one which makes the heart run over.*

SAMUEL JOHNSON

*In everyone's life, at some time, our inner fire
goes out. It is then burst into flame by an encounter
with another human being. We should all be
thankful for those people who rekindle the inner spirit.*

ALBERT SCHWEITZER

*Let us be grateful to people who make
us happy; they are the charming gardeners
who make our souls blossom.*

MARCEL PROUST

A sweet friendship refreshes the soul.

PROVERBS 27:9 MSG

Hand grasps hand, eye lights eye. . .
and great hearts expand, and grow. . . .

ROBERT BROWNING

It is in the shelter of each other that people live.

IRISH PROVERB

The unselfish effort to bring cheer to others will be the beginning of a happier life for ourselves.

HELEN KELLER

Thanks to a benevolent arrangement of things, the greater part of life is sunshine.

THOMAS JEFFERSON

In what seems ordinary and everyday there is always more than at first meets the eye.

CHARLES CUMMINGS

Every experience God gives us,
every person He puts into our lives
is the perfect preparation for the future
that only He can see.

CORRIE TEN BOOM

I have learned that to have a good friend
is the purest of all God's gifts, for it is
a love that has no exchange of payment.

FRANCES FARMER

The world is so empty if one thinks only of the
mountains, rivers, and cities; but to know someone
who thinks and feels with us, and who, though
distant is close to us in spirit, this makes the earth
for us an inhabited garden.

JOHANN WOLFGANG VON GOETHE

Unshared joy is an unlighted candle.

SPANISH PROVERB

So long as we love, we serve; so long as we are loved
by others, I would say that we are indispensable;
and no man is useless while he has a friend.

ROBERT LOUIS STEVENSON

Do all the good you can,

By all the means you can,

In all the ways you can,

At all the times you can,

To all the people you can,

As long as ever you can.

JOHN WESLEY

Whatever is lovely. . .think about such things.

PHILIPPIANS 4:8 NIV

o be glad of life, because it gives you the chance to love and to work and to play and to look up at the stars. . .to think seldom of your enemies, often of your friends, and every day of Christ. . . these are little guideposts on the footpath of peace.

HENRY VAN DYKE

Whoever is happy will make others happy, too.

ANNE FRANK

⌒

he kingdom of heaven is of the childlike,
of those who are easy to please,
who love and give pleasure.

ROBERT LOUIS STEVENSON

⌒

The best portions of a good life are
the little, nameless, unremembered acts
of kindness and love we do for others.

WILLIAM WORDSWORTH

There are many things in life that will catch your eye, but only a few will catch your heart—pursue those.

MICHAEL NOLAN

∞

Flowers are lovely; love is flowerlike. Friendship is a sheltering tree.

SAMUEL TAYLOR COLERIDGE

∞

Verily, great grace may go with a little gift; and precious are all things that come from friends.

THEOCRITUS

If you keep a smile tucked away in your heart,
it's easy to keep one on your face.

One filled with joy preaches without preaching.

MOTHER TERESA

Instead of being unhappy,
just let your love grow as God wants it to grow.
Seek goodness in others. Love more persons more. . .
unselfishly, without thought of return. The return,
never fear, will take care of itself.

HENRY DRUMMOND

Blessed are they who have the gift of making friends, for it is one of God's best gifts. It involves many things, but above all the power of going out of one's self and appreciating what is noble and loving in another.

THOMAS HUGHES

The key is to keep company with people who uplift you, whose presence calls forth your best.

ELIZABETH WILLET

Few delights can equal the mere presence of one whom we can trust utterly.

GEORGE MACDONALD

Good understanding wins favor.

PROVERBS 13:15 NIV

*Insomuch as any one pushes you
nearer to God, he or she is your friend.*

FRENCH PROVERB

*Life is short. Be swift to love;
make haste to be kind.*

HENRI F. AMIEL

Some people come into our lives, leave footprints on our heart, and we are never the same.

UNKNOWN

Kind words can be short and easy to speak, but their echoes are truly endless.

MOTHER TERESA

Love is an image of God, and not a lifeless image, but the living essence of the divine nature which beams full of all goodness.

MARTIN LUTHER

Cheerfulness is the offshoot of goodness.

CHRISTIAN NESTELL BOVEE

*The greatest pleasure I know is
to do a good action.*

CHARLES LAMB

*Is it so small a thing to have enjoyed the sun,
to have lived light in the spring, to have loved,
to have thought, to have done;
to have advanced true friends.*

MATTHEW ARNOLD

May love shine down on you always.

UNKNOWN

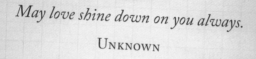

It is a comely fashion to be glad—
joy is the grace we say to God.

JEAN INGELOW

It is astonishing how short a time
it takes for very wonderful
things to happen.

FRANCES HODGSON BURNETT

Love conquers all things.

VIRGIL

Holding the heart of another in the comforting
hands of prayer is a priceless act of love.

JANET L. WEAVER

To love is to place our happiness
in the happiness of another.

GOTTFRIED WILHELM VON LEIBNIZ

Love is all we have, the only way
that each can help the other.

EURIPIDES

The one who blesses others is abundantly
blessed; those who help others are helped.

PROVERBS 11:25 MSG

Certain persons do exist with an enormous
capacity for friendship and for taking delight
in other people's lives.

WILLIAM JAMES

Nothing we do, however virtuous,
can be accomplished alone;
therefore, we are saved by love.

REINHOLD NIEBUHR

Blessed are the happiness makers;
blessed are they that remove friction,
that make the courses of life smooth.

HENRY WARD BEECHER

Life itself cannot give you joy
unless you really will it.
Life just gives you time and space—
it's up to you to fill it.

CHINESE PROVERB

Teach me, Father, to value each day,
To live, to love, to laugh, to play.

KATHI MILLS

It is pleasing to God whenever you rejoice
or laugh from the bottom of your heart.

MARTIN LUTHER

The world is a rose;
smell it and pass it on to your friends.

PERSIAN PROVERB

Friends are the angels
who lift us to our feet when our wings
have trouble remembering how to fly.

UNKNOWN

Just as there comes a warm sunbeam
into every cottage window, so comes love—
born of God's care for every separate need.

NATHANIEL HAWTHORNE

I am beginning to learn that
it is the sweet, simple things of life
which are the real ones after all.

LAURA INGALLS WILDER

There is no duty we so underrate
as the duty of being happy.
By being happy, we sow anonymous
benefits upon the world.

ROBERT LOUIS STEVENSON

It is often just as sacred to laugh
as it is to pray.

CHARLES SWINDOLL

A kind heart is a fountain of gladness,
making everything in its vicinity
freshen into smiles.

WASHINGTON IRVING

Joyfulness keeps the heart
and face young.

ORISON SWETT MARDEN

Happiness held is the seed;
happiness shared is the flower.

JOHN HARRIGAN

Count your age by friends, not years.
Count your life by smiles, not tears.

UNKNOWN

There will never be anyone like you.
Allowing God to fulfill His purpose in you
is the miracle for which you were created.

UNKNOWN

Hold a hand that needs you
and discover abundant joy.

FLAVIA WEEDN

I think I began learning long ago
that those who are happiest are those who
do the most for others.

BOOKER T. WASHINGTON

Every day we live is a priceless gift of God,
loaded with possibilities to learn something new,
to gain fresh insights.

DALE EVANS ROGERS

Celebrate yourself! You are a unique creation
of God. In all the world, there's no one else
like you. . . . Praise God for all the gifts
He gave the world when He created you.

ELLYN SANNA

Since you are like no other being ever created since
the beginning of time, you are incomparable.

BRENDA UELAND

If your heart is full from the blessings God has rained on you lately, revel in this season of joy and let your laughter reverberate to the heavens.

UNKNOWN

He is first, and He is last! And we are gathered up in between, as in great arms of eternal loving-kindness.

AMY CARMICHAEL

You are God's created beauty and the focus of His affection and delight.

JANET L. WEAVER

*The purpose of our lives is to give birth
to the best which is within us.*

MARIANNE WILLIAMSON

A cheerful heart fills the day with song.

PROVERBS 15:15 MSG

*You are a part of the great plan,
an indispensable part.
You are needed; you have your own unique
share in the freedom of Creation.*

MADELEINE L'ENGLE

Flowers preach to us if we will hear.

CHRISTINA ROSSETTI

With. . .the deep power of joy,
we see into the life of things.

WILLIAM WORDSWORTH

This is the true joy in life,
the being used for a purpose recognized
by yourself as a mighty one.

GEORGE BERNARD SHAW

All love is sweet,

Given or returned.

Common as light is love,

And its familiar voice wearies not ever. . . .

PERCY BYSSHE SHELLEY

Nothing is sweeter than love,
nothing higher, nothing broader, nothing better,
either in heaven or earth; because love is born
of God, and, rising above all created things
can find rest in Him alone.

THOMAS À KEMPIS

What I am
here is a wonderful mystery
to which I will respond with joy.

Unknown

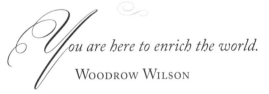

ou are here to enrich the world.

Woodrow Wilson

Gratitude is the fairest blossom
which springs from the soul.

HENRY WARD BEECHER

G od has given us two hands—
one to receive with and the other to give with.
We are not cisterns made for hoarding;
we are channels made for sharing.

BILLY GRAHAM

Charity is above all a hymn of love.
Real, pure love is the gift of oneself.

PIUS XII

You have a special place in my heart.
You share with me the special
favor of God.

PHILIPPIANS 1:7 NLT

One looks back with. . .gratitude to those
who touched our human feelings.

CARL JUNG

The heart benevolent and kind
the most resembles God.

ROBERT BURNS

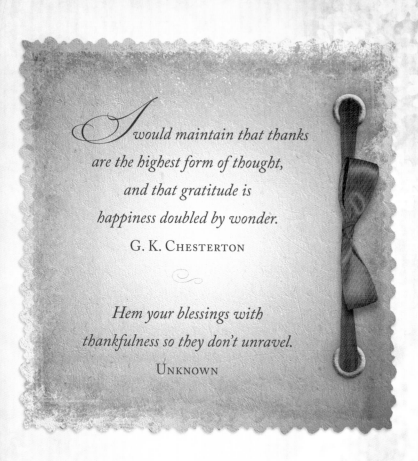

I would maintain that thanks
are the highest form of thought,
and that gratitude is
happiness doubled by wonder.

G. K. CHESTERTON

Hem your blessings with
thankfulness so they don't unravel.

UNKNOWN

*The smallest act of kindness is worth more
than the grandest intention.*

OSCAR WILDE

*How far that little candle throws
his beams! So shines a good deed
in a naughty world.*

WILLIAM SHAKESPEARE

*The art of life is to live in the present moment
and to make that moment as perfect as we can by
the realization that we are the instruments and
expression of God Himself.*

EMMET FOX

What wonderful worlds we can find in others!

EDWARD E. FORD

I have found that there is tremendous joy in giving.

WILLIAM BLACK

*Human beings ought to. . .share all
the gifts they have received from God.*

MEISTER ECKHART

Life holds so many simple blessings,
each day bringing its own individual wonder.

JOHN McLEOD

The most precious things in life are near at hand.

JOHN BURROUGHS

Prayers go up and blessings come down.

YIDDISH PROVERB

"The Lord bless you and keep you;
the Lord make his face shine upon you
and be gracious to you; the Lord turn his face
toward you and give you peace."

Numbers 6:24–26 niv

However many blessings we expect
from God, His infinite liberality will always
exceed all our wishes and our thoughts.

John Calvin

Unselfish and noble actions are the most radiant

pages in the biography of souls.

David Thomas

A loving heart is the truest wisdom.

Charles Dickens

How beautiful a day can be

When kindness touches it!

George Elliston

May there always be work
for your hands to do.

May your purse always
hold a coin or two.

May the sun always shine
on your windowpane.

May a rainbow be certain
to follow each rain.

May the hand of a friend
always be near you.

May God fill your heart
with gladness to cheer you.

Irish Blessing

*Thank you for making my
world brighter.*

*You hold a special place
in my heart—
now and forever.*